*your loving
Brother
Albert
x x x x x*

ISBN 0 904847 14 4

Reprinted 1992

The People's Press of Milton Keynes

c/o The Living Archive Project, The Old Bath House, Stratford Road, Wolverton, Milton Keynes.

INTRODUCTION

When Mabel Browne died in 1975 her daughters were faced with the task of selling their mother's house and sorting out her possessions. Among the things they got rid of was a box of her old books. I bought this box from a second-hand furniture store, and when I got home I found a bundle of old letters in it beneath the books. These letters might not have meant anything to her daughters but Mabel Browne had obviously thought they were important enough to keep them until she died. On reading them it is easy to understand why she'd treasured them. They were mostly from her brother Albert who had left home to fight in the First World War.

Mabel Browne was born Mabel French and was the eldest of four children. She and her brothers Albert, Will and George lived in Young Street, Wolverton in Buckinghamshire. Their mother had died and for some years Mabel had looked after her brothers. Eventually Miss Gates, an elderly spinster, was engaged by their father to look after them. She was called 'Aunt' by the children.

Albert Edward Mortlock French was born in New Bradwell on June 22nd, 1899 and was an apprentice engineer at the Wolverton Railway Works when he left home to enlist in 1915. He was just 16 years old. Brother George remembers him as 'tall and dark-haired looking older than he really was. He was a chap that had to shave pretty quick, so when he went to join the Army of course there was no questions about his age, he said he was 18 and that was it'.

In his spare time Albert had been a keen member of the Wolverton Church Lads' Brigade. The Church Lads' Brigade had strong links with the King's Royal Rifles – indeed the 16th Battalion of the KRR's was nicknamed the 'Churchman's Battalion' as it was raised entirely from former members of the Church Lads' Brigade. This explains why Albert went to London to join up – the Regiment's Recruiting Headquarters were in the Strand. When the family found out, Albert's father apparently tried to stop him, but he'd already taken the King's shilling.

Albert wrote home regularly mainly to his sister Mabel or 'May' as she was affectionately known. Not all of the letters are dated and I've frankly guessed which order they came in, although there are clues which have influenced my decisions. Those letters with a date reveal that they were mostly written on Sundays. Although Albert gives no definite date in his letters it appears that he left for France in early May 1916. He was in France for only about six weeks when he was killed, just a week before his 17th birthday.

Albert's surviving brothers George and Will told me that their father applied for a war pension, but the War Office refused it, apparently on the grounds that Albert had lied about his age on joining up and was under the official enlistment age when he was killed. The two brothers wrote to the local Member of Parliament who took up the case for them. Eventually Albert's father received a war pension of 5 shillings a week. George French is still bitter about his older brother's death. "He's the only one that's, that has affected me like that, I mean my own father and mother and any of them really that died. It's the way he died of course. He shouldn't have been there, should he?"

What makes the letters remarkable is that they record the subtle change of feelings that Albert underwent as his boyish enthusiasm and ambition met the harsh reality of army training and trench life. If he had survived and had been interviewed later it is extremely unlikely that these changes in attitude would have been remembered.

It is not for me to tell you the reader what quality Albert French's letters have, that is for you to decide. It is however worth pondering on the fate of that bundle of letters which had been thrown away and only rescued by accident. This publication is only the latest in a series of ways in which those letters have been used. Roy Nevitt, Director of Drama at Stantonbury Campus, adapted the letters into a musical documentary play, they are used as curriculum material in teaching about the First World War, and I used them as the subject of a BBC Radio 4 documentary. Brother George remarked during the course of that programme that he'd visited Albert's grave and that it had been the only grave he'd seen without the age of death on it. An official at the Commonwealth War Graves Commission heard the programme and offered to rectify the omission. Albert's gravestone now bears the legend "aged 16 years".

Roger Kitchen
October 1983

For God, For King & For Country

Y · M · C · A

H.M. FORCES ON ACTIVE SERVICE

PATRON
Y.M.C.A NATIONAL COUNCIL
H.M THE KING

PATRON
MILITARY CAMP DEPT.
H.R.H DUKE OF CONNAUGHT.

Dear May
Cheer up. I am coming home next Saturday.
   By the way if anybody wants to write to me, they will have to address me like the address below, in the shape of an envelope.

                     Stamp

Rifleman A.E.M. French
   K.R.R.
Regimental No. 7259 E Company
    Gidea Park
      Romford
        Essex

If you address the envelope exactly like this, it will reach me all right.
   If you or Aunt wants to know all the details, you had better read Dad's letter, because I have told him almost everything, in that letter. When I arrive home in the uniform of the King on Saturday, you will be able to take me out, and swank as you call it. The only thing is, that I shan't have any money to treat me, or myself or you or anybody else, because I shall only have enough money to pay my fare to Wolverton, and back here again. On Saturday I shall get to Euston about half-past two, and then take the first train home. So I shall arrive home some time on Saturday afternoon, in any case not later than half past five, tea time. Tell Aunt that if she has the tea early, that I should like some tea, if I get home late, as I shall not have any money to buy refreshments on the way.
      With love and good wishes until next Saturday
        Your dear brother, Albert

Y·M·C·A
Y.M.C.A.   Y.M.C.A.
H.M.FORCES ON ACTIVE SERVICE

PATRON
Y.M.C.A NATIONAL COUNCIL   MILITARY CAMP DEP'T
H.M THE KING   H.R.H. DUKE OF CONNAUGHT

Stationed at Gidea Park, Romford   *Kings Royal Rifle Corps*
Essex.   *November 6 1915*

Dear May
I have just received your letter, and being as I have plenty of time
I am going to write you a good letter. Of course, when I send a
letter to any one of you, I really mean it for all of you. I thought
perhaps when I send a letter or P.C. to any one of you, that the
others might think that I had forgotten them. Of course, I have
not time to write to each one of you, so I must write to one, and
make it do for the lot. Referring to Aunt's last letter about
arriving home safely, Aunt said that she hoped that I did not get
very wet. It did not rain at all in London that day or the next. We
have it very wet since though. In that same letter Aunt said that
Will wrote a letter, and as Aunt could not find it she would leave
it until the next letter. Will's letter was with Aunt's letter all right.
I expect that Will shoved his letter in the envelope, and forgot all
about it. The stamp was on all right, and the handkerchiefs were
all right. Thanks very much for sending the handkerchiefs quickly
because I lost the one which I took with me. A gentleman in our
room has since given me 2 nice white handkerchiefs, because he is
going to have khaki handkerchiefs. I shall get 3 khaki handker-
chiefs sometime, so that will make 7. I shall send 5 home at a time
and keep 2. We now have in our company Lord Butler's son who
is going to have a commission, a Lord's son, a Belgian Millionaire,
worth £15,000,000, the Earl of Crewe's son, and 6 well known
gentleman's valets. So you see May we have quite a lot of gentry
in our company. In Will's letter, Will asked me to get him some
cigarette photos, but as most of the fellows smoke Woodbines, I
shall not be able to get him any photos at all, He also asked me
how many Germans I shot on my route march. Tell him that we
did not see a German of any description during the whole march.
And he asked me what kind of drill it was that was going to make
me 6 ft before Christmas. Tell him that if we keep on having the
good plain food, the stiff drills, and the fresh air we are having
now, I shall not be far short of 6 ft. When I come home at Christ-
mas I shall bring him something back better than cigarette photos.

And of course I shall bring George and all of you something back as well. If you are going to send me some chocolate next week, May, I shall be very glad, and I thank you very much for it, although it has not yet come. If it did not come I should know the reason why, I know you can ill afford it. I am going to get in a better position than I am before another 3 months, and I am going to try to be a lance-corporal before Christmas. Last Friday we were short of section commanders, so the commander asked me to command one section. I had to drill them, and the commander said I was very good. He said I was getting on quick. So you see I am getting on all right, and stand a good chance of rising from the ranks. Have you had any separation money yet? If you have not, you must tell me in the next letter, and I will inquire into the matter. How is Alice at Wood Green getting on now, I hope she is as well as she can be. I hope that Mrs Cox did not mind me not going in to see her. Of course, I suppose she understood that I did not have time. Mrs Cox will have to come up and see me at Christmas when I come.

I am sorry to say that I shall not be able to go to Mrs Cope now because I shall not be able to have another pass until Christmas. When I come home at Christmas I shall get home just as quick as I did this time, although I shall be further away. When I come home at Christmas I shall have at least 6 days leave, and shall jolly well make up for not coming home now. Do not be surprised if I am about 6 ft high, as Will says. If I am Dad will have to cut a bit out of the front door, so that I can get in. We always have to wear our belts now. A battalion of the Sportmans, and a brigade of R.F.A. went to the Dardanelles from here 3 days ago. It was fine to see about a mile of guns moving along. We are going to Andover to join the 19th batt. of K.R.R. Two K.R.R. men were accidently killed by bayonet fighting at Aldershot the other day, both of them lunged together. There are 10 Scotch regiments, 3 Irish, and 6 English regiments are stationed around Aldershot. All of them have been stopped fighting with the naked blades now, and have to use their scabbards. Our fellows have an idea that we are going in billets at Andover. They say it is not a very lively place, although it is a pretty part, but we shall have to make the best of it. The 17th K.R.R. stationed at Whitley, near Aldershot, say that the nearest house to them is 3 miles away, so we shall be better off than they are any rate. Tell Dad I am going to follow up fitting and turning, study with my books when I get a case, buy a military book of some kind every week, and become a Major-General someday. When once I start going, that is after I've been made a Lance-Corporal, I shall rise like the early morn-

ing dew. You need have no fear about my looking after myself and behaving myself May, because I only go out about 3 nights a week, and then usually by myself. I either walk round the town or go to the Y.M.C.A. at Romford, where there are all kinds of games and concerts. When I stop in camp I either go in our own Y.M.C.A. and read books or war news, or sew buttons on, or have a chat with another decent fellow out of our room on military affairs. So you see I behave myself alright. I have one jolly good wash, wash my hair every day, and clean my teeth every day, and bathing parade once per week. We have to sleep on one straw mattress, pillow, three blankets, and waterproof sheet. They keep you warm, but if you wake up about 1.00 a.m. you feel slightly cold. If we go in billets at Andover I expect our beds will be better than they are now. I hope that you are all as healthy as I am. Tell Aunt that I am wearing my pants now, and they are quite comfortable now. Tell Dad that the sergeants have got me spotted for knowing my drills, signals, and semaphore, and are quite friendly with me. Next time you write will you tell me Reg's address, so that I can send him a bit of St Julien, and ask him how he is getting on. You can tell Mrs Cope that I shall send a photo if I have a chance to have any taken. Aunt was lucky to get those 2 handkerchiefs and letter through for a penny because I should have thought there was above 1 ounce there. Was the new act in force then?

Do you think that I shall be able to send 5 handkerchiefs and a letter home for a penny? If not I shall have to send two only. One handkerchief will last one week all right. I do not know exactly what it is, but just lately I have felt quite good, that is to say religious. In fact 3 others, of a Sportmans' Company, and I felt so good last night, Sunday, that we were converted at a "Salvation Army Headquarters". It is a bigger thing than being confirmed. You have your sins forgiven, and promise God not to swear, steal, lie, deceive, misconduct yourself, and to obey the 10 commandments. I have felt quite spiritual and changed since Sunday, and I do not trouble what anybody says, it is better to live as God desires you to, than to live anyhow. There are some soldiers who have an opinion that this war will be the end of the world, but whether it is or whether it is not, I have made a start for the good. I hope you do not think I am balmy, but I have told you this because I knew you would be pleased to hear it. Well I think I had better go on and talk about something else now, now I have told you all about my change. I shall write to you just as often as I do now when we move to Andover, so you will have plenty of news. I shall not be able to write much more now, because we have to attend a Chapel service tonight and another one on Wednesday. Tell Dad and Aunt to drop me a line as soon as possible. Give my love to Dad, the boys and Aunt.

From your loving Brother Albert.

x x x x x x x x x x x x x x x x x x x x x x x x x x x x x x x x x

P.S. I will write you a P.C. on Wednesday. If this letter is over-weight you will have to tell me.

For God, For King & For Country

Y.M.C.A. NATIONAL COUNCIL
PATRON
H. M. THE KING

MILITARY CAMP DEPT
PATRON
H.R.H. DUKE OF CONNAUGHT.

Stationed at Gidea Park, Essex   *November 13 1915*

Dear May
I hope that you, Aunt and Dad, and the boys are in good health,
as I am in excellent health, in fact I have never been otherwise
since I have been here. I received your parcel safely at 10 a.m.
this Saturday morning. I did not think that there would be so
much chocolate as there was, and I was highly pleased with it,
and I thank you, my dearest sister, very much for it. Of course,
I gave some of the lads in our room a piece, because they always
share their parcels, you can bet that I had the lions share of it
though. They all said that it was good stuff. We never went that
12 miles route march after all because it was so wet. We have had
it very wet on and off ever since I have been here, and our camp
and the fields round about are in an awful state. But in spite of
this, I am healthier than I ever have been in my life. We do not
take any notice of cold and wet. You get quite hardened in a
short time. But there is one funny thing about our regiment, we
never drill if it rains, unless we are under shelter. Our recruits are
still rolling up about 20 a day. But I see that they will have to
buck up if they want to avoid having conscription. Our men say
that there is not a better man going than our Captain for know-
ledge, and he says that we shall pull through this war, but it will
be a long and hard struggle. His opinion is the same as mine that
the war will be won by sheer weight of numbers. He says that if
we had 10 millions of troops fighting the Germans, we could not
break through at present, because the German positions are like
ours, impregnable. The captain says that as sure as anything the
whole of the K.R.R. will go to the front sometime. There is a
strong rumour that when we go we shall go to Serbia, because
we are the youngest and most active infantry regiment in the
British Army. There are many chaps being made Corporals and
Lance-Corporals in our regiment, but I shall not bother about a
stripe till I am a bit bigger, as there might be some jealous remarks
about my age. I have plenty of time yet, and as I have told you
before when I start going, I shall keep on rolling. Give my love to
Aunt, Dad, and the boys. I will write you all a nice long letter
tomorrow, Sunday.
With love from your dearest, loving Brother Albert.

Y·M·C·A

H.M.FORCES ON ACTIVE SERVICE

PATRON
Y.M.C.A NATIONAL COUNCIL
H.M.THE KING

PATRON
MILITARY CAMP DEP'T
H.R.H. DUKE OF CONNAUGHT

Dear May

Just a nice letter to let you know that I am quite well and all right and hope you are the same. We have had a lot of snow here, and its fearfully cold at present here, freezing all the while. The other day in a big field day we had to lay on a large plain quite still, half an hour, and there was a terrible cold cutting wind all the while. Some of the chaps were absolutely groaning with cold. I have just about got used to the different climates, and can stand a good deal of cold, but I had to exert all my powers to stand that, but you ought to have heard them as they were going back home. They were yelling all the way, "Are we downhearted No-o-o-o". And they didn't half let it rip, too. We arrived home about 10.30 p.m. that night. I expect Wolverton now is what Yorkshire men would call a wash-out, which means no use at all. So Sid Johnson is home again. I should have thought he would have known what to do with his leave, because leaves are not very plentiful. I must thank you very much for the postal order.

x x x x x x x x x x x x x x x x x x x x x x x x x x x x

I must put the rest of the news in Aunt's letter. I will write again shortly. With fondest love

from Albert

For God, For King & For Country

Y·M·C·A
H.M. FORCES ON ACTIVE SERVICE

Y.M.C.A.

Y.M.C.A.

PATRON
Y.M.C.A NATIONAL COUNCIL
H.M.THE KING

PATRON
MILITARY CAMP DEP⁺
H.R.H. DUKE OF CONNAUGHT

North Camp Aldershot

Dear May
I hope you are getting on all right now. I hope your quinsy and bad throat are better now. I hope it soon got better after it broke. It must have been very bad to have Dr Miles and a Nurse to see you. Troubles always seem to come all at once, but we must make the best of them. Well, our battalion starts its Christmas leave next Thursday. I shall very likely come home next Thursday, for at least 4 days, but I cannot say for absolute certainty. Of course, I shall send you all particulars before Thursday.
    I hope Dad, Aunt, Will and George are all quite well, as I am quite well. Well cheer up and goodbye until next Thursday.
    From your ever loving Brother Albert x x x

PATRON
Y.M.C.A. NATIONAL COUNCIL
H. M. THE KING

PATRON
MILITARY CAMP DEPT
H.R.H. DUKE OF CONNAUGHT

Dearest May

I hope you are quite well as it leaves me the same. Perhaps I shall come home at Christmas, after all. Look in Aunt's letter, for part about coming home. Well, I hope your work went down all right. We all have troubles and trials, but with a little pluck, and grit, you win through all right. We went a 16 mile route march yesterday, with packs, ammunition, bayonets, rifles, in fact we had everything. 4 miles of this march was over a boggy plain, up to our knees (without exaggeration) in sand, mud and water. Two horses which sank in the mud up to their heads had to be hauled out with ropes. Before we got back the fellows weren't half carrying on. As soon as we got our packs off and rested, the fellows were as happy as ever. We are learning shooting, and bayonet fighting now. They have been seeing about our allotment money, so you will hear of it shortly. Have you heard anything of Wilfred Saunders lately? How are the boys getting on up there? Have you had any unusual happenings at Wolverton lately? Does "Barber's Picture Palace" still go all right? Has anybody up our way enlisted lately? Are all your mates all right? I have wrote to Aunt Jane, but I have not had time to write to Reg or Mrs Cox yet. Have you heard from Reg yet? Is Mr and Mrs Cope all right? They have not had a Zeppelin raid up there for a good while, have they? Well, I will write again soon. Cheer up, and smile. With fondest love from

Albert x x x x x x x

Dear May

I hope you will not mind me not writing before. I have been so busy in the trenches, that we hardly knew what day it was. So I know you will excuse me. I expect you were all anxious, and wondering why you did not have a Christmas letter. I did send a letter on Christmas Eve, but it was not a proper Christmas letter. I scribbled it off in my spare time. I just managed to finish it. I have not had a Christmas letter yet, and it is 9.30 p.m. Christmas Sunday night now. I am expecting one any time from you now though. I know why I've not had a letter. I know you will all be very busy, the same as I was. I hope you had as happy a Christmas as possible, under the circumstances. I had a decent Christmas, but it was nothing like being at home. Still, I made a decent job of it.

If you do not receive a letter any time for a good while, you must not be anxious, you must put it down to trench digging, or night marches, or something of the sort. So you will know next time if you are a long while receiving a letter. You can expect me home within a fortnight. We are having 7 days leave. It will be a decent leave, won't it? I shall have time to have a good look round Wolverton, and have a jolly good talk.

I think I shall be able to tell you as much about soldiering as most of them. I've had two parcels, one from inhabitants of Wolverton, the other from a chap's uncle. This chap, who sleeps near me, likes me, and got his uncle, who lives at Brighton, to send me a Christmas parcel, as a kind of surprise packet. I used to be unlucky at one time, but I seem to be quite lucky since I joined the army.

With fondest loveliest love from Albert x x x x x x

For God, For King & For Country

 Y·M·C·A

H.M FORCES ON ACTIVE SERVICE

PATRON
Y.M.C.A NATIONAL COUNCIL
H.M THE KING

PATRON
MILITARY CAMP DEPT.
H R H DUKE OF CONNAUGHT.

Dear May
I hope you are all getting on all right as it leaves me the same.
I meant to write to you before, but the last two or three days,
we have been out from 8 a.m. to 9 p.m. so it was impossible. Well
I am getting on topping: today we have been on a brigade field
day round a place called "The Devils Punchbowl". It's a piece of
land about 3 miles round the top. The top is flat for about 3
yards and then slopes down to an awful depth. A sailor was
murdered there in 1756, as he was going to Portsmouth by an
highway man. They buried the sailor, and erected a stone telling
all about the barborous murder. About 50 yards away there is a
stone cross which the highwayman was hung on. The murdered
sailor was a Witney man. On another old stone near our camp its
got Portsmouth 33 miles, and Hyde Park Corner 36 miles, which
shows that we are not so far from the seaside or London. It
always seems curious to see such names on a mile stone. Well,
there are lots of old events which took place in the Devils Punch-
bowl. Its supposed to be haunted. Well we started from Camp
with our old brigade, the eight bands. They were, The Royal
West Kents, leading, then the East Surreys, Hampshires, and
18th K.R.R. We had to go last because they knew if they had us
in front we should march too fast for them. Before we had gone
2 miles 6 East Surrey and 2.R. West Kents had dropped out. They
are not used to hard work like the 18th KRR. It was an awful
crawl all the way. When we got within two miles of the Devil's
Punchbowl the 18th K.R.R. had to attack the R. West Kents,
who had white bands round their hats. We advanced in lines like a
lot of ants. When we were within 400 yards the battle began. You
cannot hardly tell the difference between these hills and khaki.
We started with our rifle fire with ball cartridge, and the machine
guns started too. The rifle fire was going bang, bang, bang crash
and the machine guns were going jip, crash, bang, rattle. There
was no big gaps fell but 2, a mile away, but there was an awful
row. There was a good deal of smoke too.
Our platoon were the reserves, laying down on top of the
punchbowl watching the battle in the valley. We had got to make
the final charge if we was needed, but we was not near. After an

hour the K.R.R. began to advance and we drove them back by our fire, and we were all over the job. The stretcherbearers were all over the place taking away the wounded men and the signallers were behind any bushes and signalling to each other. But the West Kents knew they were beaten and had to give in. So we won. Of course it was all sham fighting, although it's possible to get hurt in sham fighting. We all marched and had our dinner in a big field. We all camped together. We stayed there an hour and a half. Of course all the ladies from the neighbouring villages had to come and have a look at us, as usual. We could hear them saying "Oh, aren't they a fine lot of men". There were about 5,000 of us altogether. Then some more "Don't they look nice. Isn't it nice to see such soldiers. I feel quite nice when I'm near the soldiers". They compliment us well don't they? Then we start for home. I forgot to tell we didn't get our dinner till 3 p.m. The K.R.R. were in front. All the ladies wave their hands and throw kisses. We do the same. Whistling all kinds of the latest songs while we are marching, and singing with the bands. We went 4 miles an hour back. It was a nice steady pace all the way back, but when we were two miles from home we had to wait ten minutes for the other 3 regiments to catch us up. The K.R.R. got back to camp, dismissed, and had been in barracks about ten minutes when the others came straggling in. The captain told us we had a splendid name for marching up to now, and he wants us to stick to it. Tomorrow we are going on a test march. We have to march a certain distance in a certain time, and take in account the number of men that fall out. I thought I would tell you a bit about our field days, as I have not told you much about them. I hope you will understand the writing though. Yes my photos came well. I look a lot older and rather tall, that's all. You will just about have enough to go round, won't you? I've come out a lot plainer and better looking. I have received a letter from Reg Timms, His brother is going to enlist shortly. Tell Aunt I'll see to that allotment money. I'll jolly well see as you soon get it. I've talked to him three times about it already. Every time he says "All right, I'll see about it" and that's as far as that. If he doesn't see about it this week, I shall have to see the captain, the captain will see him, and see as he sees into the matter, and then you will have the papers and the money. Tell Aunt I'll keep on worrying them till they do send it. Tell her most of the fellows' parents are getting it, now. In the last letter I asked Aunt to send me 5/-, because we all had our money short in our company this week, and we shan't have it made up till three more weeks, and I've had to borrow 3/- off another fellow out of another company, and he

wants me to pay him back this week. Of course I shan't be able
to pay him back out of 3/6 this week, so I should be very glad
if one of you would send me 5/- this week so I can pay him back,
and we've got to get black buttons before Monday, which cost
about 1/- and I could get them as well. We can make it straight
after. I expect you at Wolverton had a bit of a Zeppelin scare.
Tell Dad I will send him a letter next. Give my love to them all.
With fondest love

from Albert
x x x x x x x x x x
x x x x x x x x x x

For God, For King & For Country

Y·M·C·A
H.M.FORCES ON ACTIVE SERVICE

Y.M.C.A.

Y.M.C.A.

PATRON
Y.M.C.A NATIONAL COUNCIL
H M THE KING

PATRON
MILITARY CAMP DEP'
H R H DUKE OF CONNAUGHT

January 23
Stationed at Witley Camp, Godalming, Surrey

Dear May
Just a letter to let you know that I received your chocolate, handkerchief and letter safe, although the parcel was addressed Hants instead of Surrey. It was my mistake. I hope you are quite well, as I am quite now. I have lost all my cold now, altogether. I don't talk thick or cough now and my throat and chest is quite all right. I think it must have been the sudden change of air. No I was not nervous when we could not find the guardroom. Some of them said "Blow the guardroom, let's get into bed". I said "Blow wandering about like lost sheep, let's hurry up and find the guardroom". We started walking back then, and we met more of the K.R.R. who had given the passes in, and they showed where the guardroom was. It was quarter to twelve when we gave them in, and it was twelve o'clock when we got into bed. Of course I enjoyed my week's furlough, especially with Violet on Saturday, and Sunday. It was nice being at home, and it was rotten having to come back here, it's such a dreary, out of the way place. But now I'm here, I shall have to stop. We are expecting to move any time. But now I'm in the army, I'm going to stick. It's not such an easy a job as you at first think, but now I'm in, I'm going to stick it, whatever happens, for the duration of the war, at any rate, and for a good while after if I feel like it. I'm out to make a man of myself, don't-cher know. Of course, I'm only a boy yet. Perhaps I shall get another leave, if we shift a bit nearer home. I expect Aunt has gone down to Mrs Cox, to see if there is any news from Violet. I might as well tell you that I rather took a liking to Violet while I was home and I hope she writes to me. My mate did not think much of my photo, I wonder what Violet thinks of it? My mate said I looked about 14, and not much like a soldier. I shan't be a soldier for another 2 or 3 years, I am only training for one yet awhile. How have the others turned out? I've asked Aunt to send me one, if she has one to spare. I am writing to Reg Timms, and Violet today.
    Didn't Will finish the letter he was writing with you.

"My mate did not think much of my photo, I wonder what Violet thinks of it? My mate said I looked about 14, and not much like a soldier"

I received one from him in Aunt's letter. So George is having medicine now then? Well I hope it does him good. Yes, send me a photo when you have them done of the group May please. Dear May the chocolate is lovely, I like the Boisellicors plain chocolate. I don't think I shall be sick, it's a good many years since I was sick. I've only given one fellow a little bit, because all my mates are on leave. Thanks very much. It makes a nice dessert after dinner. I forgot to tell you that we nearly all got biffed over by a motor lorry on Thursday. You see, it's like this. We used to have lanterns when we went night marching, and now we don't have them, because we are supposed to be doing the same as they do at the front. Well we were marching along quietly, when all of a sudden we heard a noise, and all chaps started yelling. I looked round and saw some lights going all over the show. I didn't look right round. I thought it's now or never, I didn't know which way to run. I thought the steering had gone wrong. I'd a good mind to stand where I was and chance getting biffed over, but at any rate I made a dash for the bank, with the others. Then I looked round the trolley was going about 30 miles an hour right into our chaps. If I had stood where I was, I should have been biffed over for a certainty. The officers and men were jumping about in all directions escaping by inches. All of a sudden it came to a stop. We looked to see if there was anybody under but we had all managed to get out of the way somehow. It appeared that the fellow lost his nerve when he found he was almost on top of us and rocked about all over the show, and then made a dive right into us. We was lucky that we all escaped, don't you think so? We are doing lots of skirmishing and marching about now. On Thursday after we had been route marching all day, we had to go marching to the fire trenches and skirmish about there. It's all done in full pack you know. Our captain told us he had been making a machine up to now, and now he was going to use it. Well May, keep on jogging along, we aren't downhearted yet are we, and never shall be either. I shan't have time to write the others one now because I've two more to write yet awhile. Give my love to Dad and the boys. With fondest love from   *Albert*

x x x x x x

x x x x

x x x

Y·M·C·A
H.M. FORCES ON ACTIVE SERVICE

PATRON
Y.M.C.A NATIONAL COUNCIL
H. M. THE KING

PATRON
MILITARY CAMP DEP'T
H.R.H. DUKE OF CONNAUGHT

Dear May
Just a letter to tell you that I am getting on all right. I have just about got over my coming home now. I hope I shall have a weekend's leave soon though. I've had two nice letters from Violet since I've been back, and sent her three. She says she has just got used to the girls now. She went to a music hall on Wednesday. She said it was fine. Well I hope you are quite well, as I am as well as you could be. We are having pretty stiff training here now, marching about 20 miles and sham fighting every day. I was very pleased with the chocolate you sent me, May. A gentleman Lieutenant of Yorkshire, who was in our company sent half a dozen cigarettes to everyone in the regiment. I gave mine to my mate. Since we came from Aldershot we have two fellows in our room, who are always acting the goat and making us laugh. One is an Irishman, named Sharp, we call him Sharpener. The other is a Scotsman named Kirby, who used to be a sergeant in the Scots Guard. Sometimes Kirby gets drunk, and two fellows bring him in and he comes in singing, and hardly able to stand up. The K.R.R. had to help furnish an extra guard with fixed bayonets for the East Surreys, because the East Surreys' prisoners in the guardroom got out of hand. When we are on the march the fellows of other regiments say "Don't you wish you were in the K.R.R's" They all envy us. Well I hope you are in the best health and spirits and all the rest of the rigme roll. I must close now, or I shan't get any tea. I will write again shortly.
With fondest love from Albert
x x x x x x x
x x x x x x x

For God, For King & For Country.

Y·M·C·A

Y.M.C.A.

H.M. FORCES ON ACTIVE SERVICE

Y.M.C.A.

PATRON
Y.M.C.A. NATIONAL COUNCIL.
H. M. THE KING

PATRON
MILITARY CAMP DEPT.
H.R.H. DUKE OF CONNAUGHT.

Dear May
I should have wrote you before, but I have had no time. We are firing the general musketry course now, which is also the final course. I am doing well up to now, but the results will not be decided until another week now. I am trying for the Marksman Badge. With either this all a first class shot you get 6d a day extra, which is called proficiency pay. 6d a day will be worth having. The bullets make a terrific row as they whistle through the air. At first the recoil of the rifle and explosion of the cartridge seemed to deafen and stun you. But now we don't take any notice of it. The different targets all have 4 different scores. There is a bull, which is 4, inner which is 3, magpie which is 2, and outer which is one. We've had rotten weather for the firing. Some days it has been raining and that cold that we couldn't feel to press the trigger. That 18th K.R.R. are doing about the best in the firing out of all the regiments round Aldershot. We usually fire near the East Surreys and West Kents, and my word you can see the difference in the scores.

Dear May, I wrote the above nearly a week ago, it is now Monday 27th, and we finished our musketry course this morning. In the 1st two parts I did splendid, but in the 3rd and final part, I did not do so well. The 2 first parts do not really count, so I have truly turned out a 2nd class shot. All those that did well in the preliminary parts, did rotten in the classification. Still there are hundreds in our battalion that haven't done as good as me. We had to do one practice in our gas helmets today. We had to put them on, and fire 5 rounds rapid in a minute. We had to run with them on too. Some of the fellows were spluttering and gasping for breath. As long as you stand still with them on there is not very much difference in your breathing, but there is a difference running. You have to keep on breathing through your nose, and blowing through your mouth. They are very simply made, most of them out of old shirts. They stink and smell horrible of chemicals. I think we are all going to be vaccinated tomorrow. We haven't heard anything official about going on leave at all, but you can expect me home within a week. I will let you know as soon as I hear something definite. As regards my allotment,

they've no business to stop 6d a week out of the 3/6. I'm glad
Aunt wrote about it. Will you tell Aunt that I should like another
pair of socks, very much, as I have only 2 pair any good, I shall
have to get some more handkerchiefs too. I bet Will is proud of
his khaki, isn't he? He ought to be one of the leading nuts in the
Wolverton C.L.B.

We all had to turn out the other night in the middle of the
night, for a fire. It was got under hand within an hour. If I come
home on leave, I shall very likely have to have full pack and
rifle. I will write again tomorrow if I have time. Give my love to
Dad, Will, George, Aunt, and Mrs. Cox, with the fondest love
from   Your loving brother Albert

                    x x x x x x x
                      x x x x x

P.S. You must excuse bad writing because, you know, I haven't
had much practice lately.

Dear May

I am very sorry to have had to keep you waiting so long, but I have been down butt marking and all manner of things. Really, I haven't had time. I received your postal order safe, for which I thank you ever so much. I hope the snow has melted down at Wolverton as it is here. All the fellows seem to be home on their last leave before they go out, don't they? There is talk of us having our last leave in 3 weeks time, and then going to Egypt. Last Friday it was India. So you cannot depend on it. The Cope's family are always in the wars, aren't they? I don't think Walt Grace would be much use for the army. I don't think he would stick the long route marches. I hope you soon hear from Reg, so that we know how he is getting on. Mr Fessy is lucky to get home for a fortnight, but they are not so particular about Bandsmen, as they are the infantrymen, especially infantrymen like the 18th K.R.R. Our captain told us that when we go abroad, we have got to let everybody in England know that we are out. He says none of us are to be taken prisoners, under any circumstance. So we shall go out with the consolation that we shan't be made prisoners of war, at any rate. Our Adjutant told us the history of the 1st K.R.R's in this war, by a diary from one of their officers. They got on fine until they went into action at the battle of Mons. They had a terrible share in it. They had 400 out of 1,000 men killed that day. The French retired and the K.R.R. held on for 3 hours after the French had gone. Then K.R.R. had to march 170 miles, fightiing all the way. After the Marne, the other 600 were nearly wiped out. Well as it is tea time I must now close with the fondest love from

Your loving Brother Albert.

x x x x x x x x x x x x x x x x x

For God, For King & For Country

Y · M · C · A
H. M. FORCES ON ACTIVE SERVICE

Y.M.C.A NATIONAL COUNCIL
H. M. THE KING

MILITARY CAMP DEPT.
H.R.H. DUKE OF CONNAUGHT.

Dear May

I expect the next letter you write to me will be in France. But, I must tell you I am in the very pink, and hope you are the same. I hope you had a decent time walking round London. I expect you did see some sights, I guess some, just a few. Perhaps Reg's letters are being stopped again. I might run across him somewhere in France, there's no knowing you know. If I do, I drop you a line, telling you Reg's quite safe, and all the rest of it. Our division started going out last night, Sunday. We are off tonight. Of course when you write my address will be A.E. French, A Coy, C/7259, 18th batt. K.R.R. B.E.F. France. I shall want another 2 pair of socks in a month's time, but I daresay we shall be able to get them out there. We are paid weekly out there. We have a pay book, and if we want some money, we have to apply for it in drafts. I might send some home, because it is safer at home than it is at Winchester.

I hope you send me one of your photos, May. I should like one very much. If I have a chance, I shall get my photo taken there. By the way, the first opportunity I get to come home on leave from France, I shall take it. I don't understand Dad not getting you a quarter fare ticket. I should think he thinks they'll sack him or something, if he just takes up a form to be signed. How is Flo Grace and all the rest of your mates getting on. Is Walt Grace in khaki yet? Arthur Morris is about eighteen now. I'll bet soldiering would not agree with him. Does little Wifee Saunders grow any bigger? By the way, I shall let you know how we are going on, as we go over to France. Well I must bring this letter to a close now, or the sergeant will be accusing me of not helping to strip our barrack room. I send my very best love to you, and remain

Your loving Brother
Albert

P.S. Cheers, and keep smiling.

The following is a true copy of a Will which was executed by the late No. C/7259 Private Albert Edward French 18th (Service) Battalion, Kings Royal Rifle Corps, while in actual Military Service, within the meaning of the Wills Act, 1838, and is therefore recognised as valid by the War Department.

WILL

In the event of any death I give half of my property to my father, one quarter to my sister, and the rest to Miss E J Gates, all of whom reside at

> *60 Young St*
> *Wolverton*
> *Bucks*

> *Albert E M French*
> *May 1st 1916*

May 15th 1916

Dear May

Just a letter to let you know that I am in the pink, and hope you are the same. How are things going at Wolverton? Is Wolverton still as quiet as usual? How is "Barbers Picture Palace" getting on? Do they still have full houses Mondays and Saturdays? There's no picture palaces, theatres, or anything here. The nearest Y.M.C.A. to us is a long way away but we have a village near us. The people round here don't worry about the war. The girls and women do all the men's work here, and they are a lot stronger, and hardier than English women. They are polite, and got cheek enough for anything.

The sergeant's just gave me one of your letters, and by the date it's taken 3 days to come, but I can't send this tomorrow so I shall put tomorrow's date on it. Notice how long it takes this letter to reach you. By the way, our officer told us to tell our people not to put France in the address, but just B.E.F. I don't know why this is, but obviously they have some crack idea for it. I had a letter from Violet Cox two or three days ago. Her letter was addressed to Aldershot, and then sent on from there with Aldershot crossed out and just B.E.F. on it. I've had about a dozen letters from Violet altogether, and you can guess I've sent her about 13. She is having a fine time with the Countess de Carlisle. I haven't wrote to you very much lately, but as Violet asked me in her last letter you must forgive me, but I haven't half been busy the last week, up till today Sunday. The worst of it is they don't give us enough grub to do it on. We spend most of our money on coffee, ginger beer and chocolate. We still get our 3/6 a week as yet, but that does not go very far. I shan't stop in the army after the war, it's not good enough. Our sergeant who has (censored) says the grub is good, but there's not enough of it. We don't get so much as we did at Aldershot. If you don't keep your eyes skinned, you don't get any at all (censored) the Rfm. go in permanent. The last lot had a hot time of it, too. But they managed to go through it unscathed. According to our N.C.O's, the Germans are an artful lot. We shall be popping away at the Germans pretty shortly, and as long as I don't get popped it will be alright, I guess. I wonder how many Germans Reg has popped? Aunt told me you had heard from him, and I was very glad to hear of it. I think the war will be over by Christ-

mas. *There's always plenty of aeroplanes fighting round here, and we can frequently see aeroplanes with shells bursting all round them. Once or twice we have seen raids on the firing line with about 10 aeroplanes. Everywhere we go we are billetted in farmhouses. By the way, I shall be pleased to have a photo of you as it is a long while since I saw you and perhaps I shall have my photo taken here, there's a shop the other side of the road. They all have the idea that soldiers like having their photos taken.*

Some of the French villages have shops which have English names, for the benefit of the English. Soldiers who have been out here 6 months can speak French, and some of the French can speak English perfectly. I can speak just a little French now. In most of the Y.M.C.A's at Aldershot ladies teach soldiers the French language free of charge. You can get 1d papers here with pretty well everything you want on it. On one side of the paper there are articles, and in English, opposite the English names, are the French names, which apply to the same article. Nutty idea isn't it. Most of the shop people understand English a little, but if they don't understand you they say "Me no compre", when you say thank you to them they jabber something in French which you can't understand. It rains very frequently here, I don't know whether the explosion of the shells have anything to do with it. The French money is very difficult to deal with, for a start they have half franc notes which value 5d, and I've seen about half a dozen of half-franc notes, and they are all marked different. It seems each district has its coins and notes marked different to the other districts. Tell Dad and the boys I will write to them shortly. By the way I am sending these 2 stamps as they are no use here. How is George getting on with his job? It's his birthday next Sunday isn't it? I· must go and see if I can get a bit more grub from somewhere now, or I'll go on strike.

Well, dear May, I must come to a close now, with my fondest, prettiest, beautifulest, loveliest love to you.

From your loving Brother Albert

P.S. This is a new invention for closing letters invented by soldiers.

P.S. I have just received Aunt's letter all right. Tell her that I wrote to Reg Timms 3 days ago, and that I have seen my mate who joined the West Kent several times out here.

On Active Service

**WITH THE BRITISH
EXPEDITIONARY FORCE**

Y.M.C.A. Y.M.C.A.

Dear Dad

Just a line hoping you are quite well, as I am still alive and kicking, and in the best of health, and getting on quite all right. I can tell you it isn't like home at all here, rather dull. I don't bother about the shells and snipers' bullets very much. Still, if you keep cheery you are all right. The war will have to end sometime, won't it? We have so long in the trenches and so long out. We haven't had very much fighting as yet. I hope that all the fresh troops here will make something shift. The weather goes to the extremes here. It is very hot in the daytime, and very cold at night. We sleep more in the daytime than we do at night. We have to work at night. I should think the fellows at Wolverton Works will stop there all together now they have been there so long. I hope we do have plenty of scraps with the Germans, as it's rotten being in the trenches, without firing at them. Of course we are very busy all the time, and there is very little time for writing letters. We don't see much life for they don't let us go about at all while we are in the trenches and when we are out there's only a small village near you. I should like to see some of the fellows at home. They would die, not being able to swank about and go to theatres. Still I don't mind a bit being here as long as we buck up and do something.

By the way when you see in the paper about aeroplanes being brought down by gunfire, you know it isn't gunfire that's brought them down, it's only luck. They fire all over the place when they fire at aeroplanes. I had Aunt's parcel quite alright and I enjoyed the stuff that was in it. I hope I shall be with you in a few month's time, and I hope they'll buck up and polish the war off. With regard to money anything you send to the front, if it's addressed properly, and tied up securely, you always get it all right. It's only when it's not properly addressed or insecurely tied up, that it does not reach you. But I have enough money to carry on with at present, and thank you very much for offering to send me some. Well dear Dad, I will now come to a close with the best of my love to you, and all at home.

I remain your loving Son

Albert

Dear Dad
Just a letter to let you know that I am in the best of health and
hope you are the same. France isn't very much different from
England, but it's very old fashioned and rather cold and wet
where we are. We are moving again. I don't know whether we
shall go in the firing line or not. They have had a lot of fighting,
and some of our N.C.O's have had some narrow escapes. When
the German aeroplanes try to pass over our lines, the shells
burst in dozens round them. It's hard to hit them, but we can see
them turn tail and hurry back. I see we have general compulsion
now. They mean to make sure of winning the war, but things will
have to go a bit quicker than they are now. So there's been a
row in the Fitting shop about the money. I don't blame them
getting all they can, though they would find a difference on this
job at 7/- a week. It would be all right here if we had a bit more
to eat. All the chaps are complaining about it. I'm not sorry I
came over here, but now I'm here I don't want the war to last
too long. If it's over by Christmas, I shall be satisfied. In any case,
I shall try and get a leave when I have been out here about
3 months.
    This is a letter which I wrote about 2 weeks ago, and I just
found it.

June 4th 1916

Dear May
I am writing to you again at last hoping you are in the pink as it leaves me the same and in the best of health. We are having it very quiet here as yet, and I wish it was more lively. The parcel Aunt sent was grand, and I thank you very much for the sweets and chocolate.

Everything here in the way of eatables and sweets are twice as dear here as what they are in England and not half so good in quality, it's hardly worth wasting your money on the stuff.

Everything is twice as dear as they are in England, except cigarettes, and ali the stuff is of rotten quality. France is no match for England. I think your photos were grand May, I've never seen anyone come out better. My mates said it was a lovely photo. We are quartered in "Musty Villa", which is the name given to our dug-out. We have to do our grub up securely, or half of it disappears to the rats and mice. But they aren't half so lousy as some people make out they are. We're having a rather warm time now, but that helps to keep you alive, We have just about got used and comfortable in our dug-out. Other of our dug-outs are called "Hotel de Ratty", "The Happy Family" and the "Abode of Love". I think our leave will start in about 2 months time. So all the soldiers have gone from Wolverton. They didn't stop long did they? There will be a few men left at Wolverton, won't there, if no more are to go from the Works. Yours and Will's birthdays, will soon be here won't they, and mine also. Our birthdays come pretty close together don't they? The shells do not make so much row as I thought they would. They make a whirling tearing noise and scream slightly. You can hear them rush through the air, but you can't see them going. They make a big hole and plenty of smoke when they burst, and bits fly about 50 yards. The bullets make a long drawn out pinging noise. Well dear May must now come to a close with the best of my love to you.

Your loving brother
Albert
x x x x x x x x
x x x x x x x x

60 Young Street
Wolverton
Bucks
6.6.1916

Dear Old Albert
Just a line hoping it finds you in the pink as usual.
We have just had the sad news to say Lord Kitchener has been drowned, my word we hadn't need lose men like him but still I expect it can't be helped. I expect Aunt told you about Reg I haven't heard since, and then only to say he was in hospital, and didn't say what was the matter with him, but I should think it must be something very bad or they would not have brought him here.

Well Albert you liked the photo then, Aunt did not, she said it wasn't like me, but every one else did and I did myself more than any I have had. Well Old boy how is the weather out in France, it has been wet here all the week-end, and Monday and today.

None of us here have got any holidays nor the school children. So it will seem a funny holiday. I might go to Bedford on Saturday or Sunday just for a change. The young boys here aren't half having to go up and enlist and some have gone to France today to work on the railway. Dad and the boys send their love, you will soon be sweet 17 and never been kissed on the 22nd of this month. Well cheerio and keep on smiling. I will close now with all my fondest love. Hurry up and send me a line as you know you owe me one. By the way Albert send us a card if you have a chance to get one as they are so pretty.

Your loving Sister
May

Mr E French

Sir
I regret to have to report the death of your son C7259 Rfn.
A. French, who was killed by machine gun fire, whilst with a
working party June 15th 1916. He was a very good soldier,
although so young, and a willing worker, who made many friends
in the company. He is sadly missed not only by his section, but
by his platoon and company, and not the least of all by myself.

The Officers, Warrant Officers, Non-Commissioned Officers,
and Rfn. of 'A' Coy 18th S.B. K.R.R.C. wish to convey to you
and your family, their deepest sympathy in this your sad bereavement.

Yours faithfully
R Pennell, Capt. for
Major
Cmdg. 'A' Coy.

122nd Infantry Brigade
B.E.F.

June 17th '16

Dear Mr French
I am very sorry to have to write to you and inform you that your dear son was killed in action on June 15th. He died as every true soldier wishes to die - doing his duty nobly for King and Country. He was doing some sand-bagging on the parapet of the trench when four bullets from a machine gun hit him, and he died instantaneously.

He lies buried amid brave comrades in a wood, and his grave is carefully tended by his friends in his battalion.

I offer you my deepest sympathy and pray that Almighty God in his mercy will give you comfort and strength to bear up under this great blow.

May I remind you of that text which occurs in the 15th Chapter of St. John's Gospel and the 14th verse? - "Greater love hath no man than this, that a man lay down his life for his friends".

I am

Yours sincerely
M.A.O. Mayne
C of E Chaplain

"He lies buried amid brave comrades in a wood, and his grave is carefully tended by his friends in his battalion"